A POETRY ANTHOLOGY

Timeless Voices

Dawn Henthorn, Sue Hylen, Diane Moser, Adelia Ritchie,
Nancy Taylor, and Beverley West

Bainbridge Island Press

A POETRY

Timeless

ANTHOLOGY

Voices

Dawn Henthorn, Sue Hylen, Diane Moser, Adelia Ritchie,
Nancy Taylor, and Beverley West

Bainbridge Island Press

Bainbridge Island, WA

Timeless Voices: A Poetry Anthology
Copyright © 2024
All rights reserved

Published in 2024 by Bainbridge Island Press
Bainbridge Island, WA
https://bainbridgeisland.press

Printed in the United States of America

ISBN: 978-1-961451-07-0
Library of Congress Control Number: 2024948270

Cover & Book Design: Ben Rockwood
Cover Image: Donna Fecteau

9 8 7 6 5 4 3 2

To Nancy Rekow,
a Bainbridge Island Treasure,
our much-loved mentor.

—Adelia Ritchie

Contents

AMOUR

WELLNESS

WHIMSY

GAIA

COMPANIONS

BACKROOM

CLIMATE

PALETTE

MEET THE AUTHORS

A POETRY ANTHOLOGY

Timeless Voices

My muse waltzes in
I pick up my pen and write
shadows disappear

—*Sue Hylen*

Introduction

The authors of the poems presented in this anthology have been friends for years. We first met in the late Nancy Rekow's writers' workshops, which she held in her large living room on Bainbridge Island, WA, on Tuesday afternoons and Thursday evenings for many years. When Nancy passed away in 2021, it was a devastating loss for all of us. We no longer had a mentor, a gathering place, a beloved and often curmudgeonly editor, or a safe place to practice and learn.

Undaunted, we continued to meet in our homes, to share and critique our poems and essays, and to support and encourage each other. Together we published *An Ode to Nancy Rekow*, an anthology chapbook of poems dedicated to our mentor, celebrating our journeys under her skilled and loving tutelage.

Then, in the summer of 2022, when I moved to Costa Rica, we decided to continue our weekly sessions on Zoom, through which the dark and lonely times of COVID had taught us how to stay connected. To this day, we meet on alternate Tuesdays, reading our works and supporting each other through technology. With an occasional *"Can you hear me now?"* or *"I can't see your face!"* we muddle through, tech-challenged, but determined, women of a certain age.

We recently realized that collectively we have an enormous body of outstanding work and that we should expose ourselves—and our favorite poems—to the world. We each agreed to submit our ten best poems, then figure out if there might be an overall theme or two, maybe send in more poems, then edit, delete, add, subtract...and *voilá!* This anthology was born.

We hope you enjoy our outlook on the world. We share some of our most personal and private aspirations, observations, dreams, experiences, and a bit of humor—in honor of that well-known poet who once told me, *"I don't write funny poems."* We hope our works also resonate with you.

—*Adelia Ritchie*

ROOTS

A poem in the night
quiet as a late snowfall
I build a bonfire
—Adelia Ritchie

There's an Old Trunk in the Attic

unopened for decades
full of dog show ribbons
desert sage from Sufi camp
worry beads & camping gear
a speckled stone from his farm in France —
locked tight, it keeps its secrets.
She kneels before it
key in hand —
lock rusty, stiff —
gray dust thick with time.
Sensing her presence,
the old trunk shivers.
A lone fly buzzes her ear.
Moisture blooms above her lip,
her cheeks scalding pink.
Sun arrows through the skylight
illuminating snow clouds of dust,
spiderwebs, half-eaten insects.
Her breath stirs the stillness.
She flips the lock open
and lifts the lid.
Her eyes close —
perfume of sage,
mustiness of aged paper.
Hundreds of thin blue airmail envelopes —
from Frankfurt, Paris, Strasbourg —
his familiar scrawl decorates.
A hot tear drops, sculpting
a tiny crater in the dust.
The ghost of her father
begins to speak.

— Adelia Ritchie

The Attic Visit

An attic, dark and mysterious
a place to hide away
things no longer needed,
or tell too much.

Next to the brick, fireplace chimney
stands a trunk with brass lock
to keep things quiet, secrets
from another time.

Inside, tissue paper wraps a wedding veil,
yellow with age and disappointments.
A baby dress and booties
still smelling of powder.

Grandma's crocheted chair covers,
so out of style,
too labor intensive
in today's world.

A photo album
full of trips
and babies
long gone.

Now sixty years later
she closes the lid
sits for awhile
then slowly walks downstairs.

— *Diane Moser*

Jessie

It was only her shell, her pod,
her physical body that carried
those arms to pull me
into her pillow breasts,
to hug me hello
and goodbye.

Her voice that spoke sage,
and soothed my cries
or—just because.

Her eyes that smiled love
when she saw me,
her lips brushing my brow.

Here—just the lifeless flesh.
She is within me now.

I hear her voice calling long distance,
"Hello! This is Grandma."

— *Dawn Henthorn*

Mom Went to Have a Baby

When I was five Mom went to have a baby
and left us with a strange lady.

My bedroom was very scary; I hoped for a girl to divide
my vigil of two doors and closet where monsters could hide.

My brother's shared their
room I did not think it fair.

When Mom called to say, *It's a girl!*
I wondered if she'd have my curls.

Our new sister's name, Barbara Lynn Baird.
I pirouetted on the kitchen floor, arms in the air

over and over annoying the lady
till our parents came home without our new baby.

We ran to the door asking to see,
Mom turned to Dad, then had to flee.

They returned shortly with a game plan,
"A hole in her heart carried her to God's hands."

Her burial too private for us to understand
years later we saw her headstone carved with a lamb.

Annually on her birthday, Mom would say,
Barbara would be XX years old today.

— *Nancy Taylor*

The Language Barrier

It was a dark and stormy night
on their return from post-war Japan.
Just three years old,
she wanted to make a very good impression
on her Most Honorable Southern Ancestor,
invoking her deepest bow.
 "Takasan ami, neh?" she said
in poor imitation of her Japanese tutors.
"Much rain, yes?"
Her parents beamed with pride
at their precocious daughter.
 "How dare you allow
my only great-grandchild
to associate with those barbarians!"
her great-grandmother spat.

— *Adelia Ritchie*

My Grandmother's Front Room

was as austere as she,
who raised four kids on a farm
during the Great Depression.

Braided throw rugs on wooden
floors provided no insulation
for the drafty house. When we asked
her to turn up the heat,
she said, *That's what sweaters
are for*.

Her furniture was for sitting,
not reclining or cushioning one's tush.
Mahogany side tables adorned
with tatted doilies lacked
a lead crystal candy jar
with sugared orange slices
like our great aunt displayed.

The legendary barn was torn
down when the acreage was sold
for a housing development.
Behind that barn,
Grandpa drank whiskey
with his sons on leave from WW2.

Behind that barn, my teetotaling Grandma
fought with her oldest son on his last leave
before the plane he piloted
was shot down.

— *Nancy Taylor*

A Raw Nerve

The hole in my gut
a raw bleeding piece of meat
nerve endings on fire gutted—
yet walking, thinking, smoking.

Nothing to say
mind spinning
in its dark cage
unable to comprehend.

What is this Thing
that leaves me so vulnerable
spiraling back to old hurts
in the ancient pit of memory.

Not good enough,
pretty enough, smart enough
unable to trust my own feelings
disapproving looks
disappointment, worry.

The father said why did you have to wear *that*?
here, let me comb your hair
the mother said you don't really feel that way
you don't think *that*.

You should do this should do that
should, should, should
looks of disapproval
disappointment, worry.

Enough.

— *Dawn Henthorn*

Anna

They couldn't find her.
That barren room with
twin bed, plywood chest
and the family rocker
was empty. Her leather purse
lay at the foot of her bed.

They looked hard;
in the small dining room
where she took her meals,
in the sparse TV room
worn chairs all empty
save for the old man
asleep in a shabby wingback.

They looked into the excuse
for a garden, weeds pushing
through the junipers
and then down the road
they found her
walking along the I-90
cardboard suitcase in hand.

At eighty-four years old,
miles from her small life,
she was going home.
No one told her
she was already there.

— *Diane Moser*

A Little Taller, a Little Fairer

After a busy workday, I stroll my grocery cart
with my toddler seated and grabbing
whatever he can reach from shelves.
I open some finger food
for him and rounding an aisle
we nearly plow into a short, young man clad in teal scrubs.
My son reaches toward the man and hollers,
"*Daddy!*"

The man's blush appears through dark skin.
I recognize this intern from the hospital
where I work. Flustered, I apologize,
he shrugs. But the tragedy here
is my little guy misses his daddy,
sees him in a stranger. While our separation
hasn't been long, his recall grows vague.
His real father is a little taller, a little fairer,
but he wears those same scrubs.

— *Nancy Taylor*

Hard to Lee!

Dad shouts
then
shoves
the Mary K's
thick wooden tiller
through
huff-blustering winds
over
Puget Sound's
silver
swirling
waves.

His hazel eyes
beam
through
my hazel eyes

our
sandy brown hair
blowing wild

our
backs & butts
stretch
over
starboard

white
water
gushing
through
shadows & light.

—*Sue Hylen*

While Knitting a Cable Knit Sweater

She is a repertoire
of
good humor
&
bad dreams

casting on
more stitches
to decrease
the tension.

knit one
purl one
cast over

in blue rage with red eyes
her pattern continues

without dropping a stitch
she pauses
to scream out the window

In real life I loved you!

—Sue Hylen

Sauk City Road
On a Back Road off Highway 20 East

Chinook winds
bend
cottonwoods & alders
against a wet
silver sky.

Glacial snow melts
as the Skagit River rises
gushing mud
knee-high
through summer cabins.

From a cliff home
he watches
old growth cedars
uproot, then float
as thunder quakes
through
this mid-January afternoon.

In August
7 a.m. rays parch
a cloudless summer sky—
a red Chevy rig
blaring
Summer Time Blues
pulls up to the site
caps a stained thermos
then waist straps his tools
to haul half-inch plywood sheathings
then hammer ten-penny nails

until 4:35pm
when he snaps the metal box latch
slams up the tailgate
pulls out to Blackie's Tavern
to swig down a Bud

talking
fish
women & rain.

—Sue Hylen

Stone to Water

The relationship with his daughters
was like water on stone.
They touched his hard defense
with a soft rolling wave
that left him open.

He had never understood
what love could be
without lust,
without wanting more.

He now understood that soft
was alright and became
more himself
than he had ever been,
then grew in the knowing.

— *Diane Moser*

JOURNEYS

phantom dreams of past
paint pictures of her long life
the world spins quickly
— Diane Moser

What's in a Name?

Don't think I'm cliché,
a nurse named Carmen cupped
me into being in the trenches of her hands.

Don't think I'm not a natural fighter,
descendant of the warring Scots,
I've vanquished every other name—
>   Deborah gored
>   Julie slashed
>   Tammy bayonetted.

Don't think my blood flows
only inside, a sanguine river spurted
from my head when jumping on a bed.

Don't think I never lived
outside of myself, as a nurse
I nurtured for thirty years.

Don't think I haven't been
wounded, my body bares seams
from staples and catgut.

Don't think I'm not made
of substance,
deep inside I claim titanium.

Don't think that I disclaim
my middle name Jane,
I favor the letter J—
>   for the virtue of Justice,
>   for the Jungle and its milieu,
>   for red tulips in June.

— *Nancy Taylor*

Year After Year

The anchor was so heavy
so weighted down
it would take death
to lift it.

Dancers of the dervish
come together year after year,
whirl around and around
heads spinning
on a projection that doesn't stop.

Do they have hope for a change
in their pattern?
Do they think
it will make a difference?

Whirl... whirl... whirl

Their lives go on
anchored to the spin
year after whirling year.

— *Diane Moser*

Brown Shadows of Sleep

hide under my eyes
I could swim to shore in them

     or

rise to the shape of a star
there is a message in shadows
perhaps the heart of a memory

     or

loss of that blanket of sleep
that rubs against the sky

     — Diane Moser

September 28, 1991

Today Miles Davis
 put his flesh
 on the note
 put that note
where it belonged.

The Man with the Horn
folds back morning
across the Sound.

At the library I scan
Dr. Seuss's obituary—
The Cat in the Hat
is gone.

In this cool air-creased
with dry leaves,
I return to sweep cobwebs
from ceiling corners
then begin to sew
a Spanish dancer's dress
for my 7-year-old daughter, Stephanie,
the Halloween of her dreams.

Later sisters Catherine and Stephanie bake cookies,
a half cup of salt in the batter!
Pay attention! Pay attention!
I say as I sew
a seam on the wrong side of the fabric.

Voices grapple at the edges,
pinking shears
keep red threads from unraveling
as the smell of cut grass swells,
yearning for a ritual
through the open back door.

— *Sue Hylen*

While Waiting to Read my Seattle Metro Bus Poems

at the Elliott Bay Bookstore Reading

My fingers trace the mortar
along these wall-pasted red bricks.
A fluted green smoke-glass lamp
illuminates
Thank you for Not Smoking.
The room converges
with poets, artists, name tags, programs
and extra folding chairs.
The mic is poised
over the podium,
framed by a blank screen.

Below this light blue
basement ceiling
are thousands of authors
with millions of words.

I have two poems to read tonight—
forty words in the second poem
sixty-one in the first.
As the room begins to hush

I see my poems
riding the buses tonight
somewhere in Seattle.

While I wait
someone
will find
my words.

—*Sue Hylen*

Quick Quick Slow

A Tango
but, where's the passion

A Waltz
just keep your distance

Covid
you come, you go, you're back again

We're tired of
this dance

No wonder no one is
doing the Polka anymore

—*Dawn Henthorn*

Double Exposure

In the middle of a dream
Mt. Rainier erupts
into the pounding Atlantic
as *Live Free or Die* cars stall,
bumper to bumper on New Hampshire
Route 1-A South, hailing
a blue moon morning
on the Isles of Shoals.

Beyond Murden Cove
gulls soar into thin sky,
like a lifetime of my father's kites,
now free on broken strings
over Puget Sound, over Rye Harbor

over my brothers searching
for sand crabs
and starfish in the blink
of White Island's lighthouse.

—*Sue Hylen*

Unspoken

Beneath the One Man Family façade
another story lifts its head,
creeps into wall-papered rooms
where young daughters sleep,

always alert to the quietest of sounds,
muscles in their bodies ready
for the mask of invisibility,
ready to go dead inside.

The tick of an alarm clock
keeps time to his breath,
as a distant train
thrusts itself down the track.

The night grows quiet again
over the patriarchal barbeque
that would host family picnics
in the safe suburban day.

—*Diane Moser*

Centrum 2019
Port Townsend Writers' Workshop, Fort Worden State Park

Beneath this majestic Madrone
      with twisted
           tangerine
                cinnamon brown limbs
                    stretching long and wide
      swallows swirl
           dip & glide
                around me.

Queen Anne's Lace
      peak through
           tall
                brown green
                  waving
                    grasses.

Setting sun paints
      rainbow shadows
           over Fort Worden's
              blinking Light House
      reflecting
           Whidbey Island's
              sandstone cliffs.

Time to go to The Reading.

—*Sue Hylen*

Midwinter, New Hampshire, 1967

Night full on her neck
she laces the belt of Orion
up her spine,
fist clenched tight
inside her pockets,
arms around her waist.

Step by step
she circles backward
up the black-glazed drive
tracing Cassiopeia and the Lion
chin to the sky.

A thick cold
bleeds a thousand dreams
in her wet eyes,
her cheeks flush white
against a red wool collar.

—Sue Hylen

A Blackened Sky

There are indelible moments in life
that stay, long after others fade away.

The water at night
was dark and endless.
It pulled everything under.
It blackened the sky,
strangled the stars
drowning them in the lake.

Tension rocked
the small wooden boat
fell over the oar lock
down, down into the deep
and sent shivers
up the young girl's backbone.

They sat stiff and alert,
locked in a spiral
of competitive emotions.
His hand a fist
with no direction.
Afraid to touch, to stoke the fire
that would quickly
turn to ashes.

Endings come in all shapes,
some quiet,
some with fire and thunder,
this one under a blackened sky.

— *Diane Moser*

AMOUR

Gentle hands entwine
silent words between two hearts
love's unspoken dance
—Adelia Ritchie

She Wasn't Young

She wasn't young, she knew the score.
She'd like, she'd lust, she'd feel the heat
but she'd never been in love before.

The men she'd known were just a bore—
her last was puffed up with conceit.
She wasn't young, she knew the score.

To men, she'd say, "*Mmmm, je t'adore.*"
She'd entertained the Royal Fleet!
But she'd never been in love before.

She'd tried them all, let them explore,
checked out each man's balance sheet.
She wasn't young, she knew the score.

Her looks attracted men galore —
she'd tossed them out like rotten meat —
'cause she'd never been in love before.

But when that man came through her door
she knew he'd make her life complete.
She wasn't young, she knew the score,
and she'd never been in love before.

— *Adelia Ritchie*

Older Lovers: Paris, 1953

A man and a woman,
he balding and scrawny,
she bulging at the waist,
share a Gauloise
while sitting, wet,
at the edge of the swimming pool
by the Seine.

He inhales,
black eyes on hers,
smoke still in his mouth and throat—
passes the cigarette to her lips.

She smiles her thanks.
I know she sees only him.

I also know,
when I'm in my 40s
I will return to Paris.

— Beverley West

A Late Romance

I hate to cook—
eat tuna sandwiches standing up,
looking out the kitchen window.

"You never cook!" my ex used to say.
"If I want a square meal
I have to make it myself!"

After the divorce,
at a Quaker meeting
I talked with a widower,
a soft-spoken man, who said,

"My wife always cooked—superbly.
In all those years we had only one problem—
she never allowed me in the kitchen."

"Oh, how sad," I said.
"Maybe come over for a visit this afternoon?
About 5:30?"

— *Beverley West*

Illicit Love

It's time to go, the hour is near.
I love you, girl, you're my best friend,
but she must never find you here.

We've known each other many a year,
through ups and downs and 'round the bend.
Now it's time to go, the hour is near.

We're a perfect fit, that much is clear.
It's difficult to comprehend,
but she must never find you here.

I pace the floor 'til you appear,
and wish our time we could extend
but it's time to go, the hour is near.

You know that I am quite sincere—
the two of us a perfect blend—
but she must never find you here.

Our love is true, you mustn't fear,
but I'm not free, I can't pretend.
It's time to go, the hour is near.
She must never find you here.

— *Adelia Ritchie*

Night Shroud

The nights stretch into infinity. Why do I care what he thinks of me? Old memories creep into restless sleep. I toss and turn as regrets burn a hole in my soul, in the heart that I left, but thought I had kept. I haven't wept and haven't slept. I didn't see, couldn't see, the truth that was right in front of me. How long? How long will I feel this way? Evening mist descends to close the day, to shroud my world. Beneath it, I'm curled like a bear in its cave. Or is it a grave?

—Adelia Ritchie

Wasted Hearts and a Full Moon

I couldn't open my heart
I wanted to
I tried
I thought I tried

Now looking back
I see
it closed down years
decades ago

And you couldn't
open yours to me either
wasted hearts
when was the sign a sign?

—Dawn Henthorn

Late Night Cuppa

In over 20 years of serving burnt coffee
to late-night drunks, she had never felt
such a body slam to her amygdala,
having felt only numbness for too long.

His musky scent invaded her nostrils and lungs,
metastasizing through her like earthworms
sliding through rich damp soil.
His look told her everything she needed to know.

Her steady hand moved toward him.
Heaving a sigh, she poured him another cup.

—*Adelia Ritchie*

Scotch on the Docks

Damn. The tissue box is empty again,
she whined, reaching instead for her Scotch.
Arianna had always preferred spiced rum
until she met Rafael,
the handsome Tico standing on the dock,
alone, in the rain.

Like the condensation on her icy glass,
tears flowed down her cheeks.
Watching Rafael sail away,
she felt as empty as that tissue box.
She turned back to her Scotch.

"Hello, do you need a hanky?"
offered the handsome stranger.

— *Adelia Ritchie*

When He Sang to Her

Her heart was a deep dark dry well
No tears left for tomorrow
No laughter for today
She merely wanted someone
To take the pain away.

But when he sang to her that night
"You fill up my senses…"
She warned him, "Be careful!
Someone could fall in love with you!"

His sunshine smile lifted her spirits
His voice was molten dark chocolate
His song sent shivers up her spine
His warm hugs thawed her frozen heart.

—*Adelia Ritchie*

The French Lesson

One taste of that frothy cappuccino
at Maxim's that April afternoon
changed her life.
Her father had taken her there
to teach her how to flirt properly.

*"The very next woman who passes us by
will fall in love with me,"* he predicted.
"Observez-moi, ma petite."
Their eyes met, he smiled.

The old woman flushed, straightened, smiled shyly,
touched her hair, and moved past us with grace.
"So, my dear, now it's your turn."

—Adelia Ritchie

WELLNESS

The climate heats up
new virus—can we adapt?
herd immunity
—Adelia Ritchie

Pager Days

It decreed our days and sometimes
our nights, whether we slept, how long
we dreamt. Attached or latched to pockets
or belts, we felt it buzz, heard it beep.
Its screen displayed call-back numbers.

It lacked complexity of gadgets today,
yet, fell in the toilet, and worked when wet!
That garage-door-opener-size pager
didn't lose a beep.

One day after inserting a patient's IV,
the doctors asked for another line.
The patient had AIDS in early days
when little was known about the disease,
even less about linked mental disorders.

When attempting to insert a second I.V.,
the frightened man's eyes gyrated,
his emaciated body summoned
supernatural strength and

he leapt out of bed grabbing me,
needle dangling mid-air.
Somehow, I escaped. Rattled,
back in my office, I hurled
my pager, and ran home and showered
till the water ran cold.

—*Nancy Taylor*

Superficial

A young woman seeks treatment
for a bloody gash on the back
of her forearm. Her extremities
remind me of birch bark.
In the interest of time,
I consider a running stitch—
in, out, in, out, then knotting
the end. But will she yank out

the single suture in the parking lot?
So, I puncture, pull, tie each stitch,
adding another seam to the teen
as the clock tick-tocks
my lunch break away. When I ask
what she thinks about as she cuts,
she says she thinks about

how she hates her dad. Adds
the pain gives her a release.
An urgent counseling appointment
is arranged but I doubt
she'll attend and fret my inept,
fix is too superficial—her injury
much deeper than I can sew.

—*Nancy Taylor*

Urgency

On Virginia's eastern shore,
a Latino man seeks care
at a migrant worker clinic.
With rabies rampant in this region,
our eyes bulge like hernias
when the man recounts
a mid-day raccoon attack.

Procurement of the vaccine,
necessary for our patient's survival,
turns into a Ping-Pong game
between the abysmally
funded free clinic and
the county health department
who stocks the pricey serum.

The patient's nationality at issue—
I plead with the health department,
the attacker is American.

       —*Nancy Taylor*

Peeing into the Abyss

When a heart
doesn't beat
one can peek
into the darkness
that might follow.

Just a clue, that's all
I ask. I want to know
what's on the other side,

but the med tech
has other plans,
pumps a gallon
of fluids into my vein.

Oh no. I must pee!
Hole in my undies,
my mother warned me
this would happen.
"Nice undies, just in case."

What did he think would happen
on the hour-long ride
to the emergency room?
"Doc, I MUST PEE, *NOW*!"

Find a bucket,
unstrap from the gurney
unhook monitors
pull blanket over his head
so I couldn't see him.

I would have peed in my boot
if it came to that.
But, instead of a peek,
I pee-e-e-e-ed
gleefully into the abyss,

reminding the Grim Reaper
to keep his umbrella handy.

—Adelia Ritchie

Dementia

Little pieces
slowly slip away
Tick Tock
Tick Tock

They blend together
like warm butter,
become words on a burnt page
holes wider by the minute.

A wordless voice
calling an unrecognized name.
Is it mine?

A little of life leaves, unobserved.
Grab the word
hold it tight
before it runs away

—*Diane Moser*

Waiting Room

The silent sound of crepe-soled shoes
fills the hospital corridor.
Shoes made for tired shifts
tending critical needs
of hope and pain.

The smell of unnamed fluids
mixed with disinfectant
wafts past the waiting room.
Families sit in stuporous silence,
resigned to wait beneath a clock
whose hands have taken a holiday.

I watch surgeons drift in and out.
Family faces reflect their news.
My mind runs in starts and stops
holding on to hope one moment,
gut-wrenching fear the next.

I stretch out my cramped leg
and wait for answers.

—Diane Moser

Promise of Tomorrow

The first time cancer appeared
I howled like a wounded dog.
No longer invincible
No longer safe
Innocence gone
Sliced away with a dull knife.

The second time
I wrote letters to dear ones
Notes of love
And buried memories
Gratitude dribbling
Down the page.

Now I wait
Submit to yearly visits
In cubicles adorned
With cheery artwork.
Pictures that promise
Tomorrow.

—*Diane Moser*

Maintenance

At this time of Life
indignities reign
sometimes I think
they hurt more than pain.

There is one thing
I ask right along
PLEASE don't you let
me die on the John.

C-pap and hearing aids
a blood pressure cuff
then arthritis and heart pills
Six more that's enough.

Salve for my foot rash
more for my knees
my hands are not working
have trouble with keys.

In thinking it over
my wish is not long
just PLEASE don't you let
me die on the John.

—Diane Moser

Mammogram

Routine screening
half naked
breasts smashed
between hard plates
tender cool hands
move flesh
to next position

x-ray humming
Frankenstein's lab sounds

Uh-oh. Grim faces
Another look
left side only
smash, move, smash, move

Humming sounds
like angry beehive
wait, wait, wait

now a sonogram
lying on table
cold, exposed
warm gel spreads
like fat slug trails

a second opinion
a third opinion
biopsy scheduled

Now we wait.

—Adelia Ritchie

Mammogram II

Worry, worry, fret and stew—
not so healthful, she well knew—
but days are tense and nights are fraught.
Such panic this small speck has brought!

Room so chill, their hands so cold,
be very still, do what you're told,
turn left, don't breathe, her eyes shut tight,
a whirr, a pop, a stinging fright.

Bits of tissue on display,
and now they need one more x-ray.
But in the end, there's naught to fear.
Biopsy reads completely clear!

—*Adelia Ritchie*

Corona Cocoon
somewhere in 2020

Sounds like a vacation spot
south of the border,
        but it's not.

I'm embarrassed to say I
really don't mind
staying home quarantined—
no appointments
no responsibilities to others,
that is, except for checking in
with friends and family,
brushing my teeth,
the occasional bath
as we reassure each other
"we're fine—just fine"
whether we are
        or not.

Sharing news of our weed-free gardens
our blooms
our little successes at organizing
cleaning a cupboard a closet—
until there's
        nothing left to share.

Not sharing our fears,
concerns,
annoyance with spouse
not *having* to go anywhere
not *having* to do anything
wrapped in our
own individual cocoons
a fairly certain outlook
we're going to make it.
　　　We're fine. Just fine.

—Dawn Henthorn

WHIMSY

Apple drops from tree
Newton names it gravity
my breasts start to sag
—Nancy Taylor

Sometimes I Wonder

why don't clouds fall from the sky
why are leaves green
what makes the wind blow
why are there rainbows
Sometimes I wish
I could see through the earth
breathe underwater
soar without wings
walk on the moon
Sometimes I hear
the sound of falling stardust
the moon laughing at earth
mountains breathing
oceans crying
Sometimes I remember
hot sand on a tropical beach
the taste of French butter
the aroma of Dad's cigar
the warm scent of you
Sometimes I wonder
where does the other sock go to hide
what became of my childhood friend
where are all those people
I gave directions to

—*Adelia Ritchie*

Walking in Sorrento, 1957

Italy is beautiful, but
oh, so hot—
one block to the pensione
and a bath—
don't know if I can
walk another step

and the sweat on my forehead
drips into my hair
I must look a fright

too hot for a girdle
so my stomach sticks out
and a run in my stocking

that guy on the bicycle
looking at me
must think American girls are
all fat—
with messy hair
sweaty armpits

he's even getting off his bike
standing there
leaning on the bike
staring
wish I'd never
left home

what's he saying?
he's shouting, *"bella, bella, bella"*

guess I don't need a bath

    — *Beverley West*

On the Bus: Seattle, 1990

The cane is lumpy,
gnarled like the hands
that grip the white pole.

She changes seats,
moves nearer the door
her backbone a triangle.

Is that bamboo? I ask.

It's briar,
real English briar.
It was my husband's.

It's beautiful, I say.

She rubs a huge-knuckled
thumb along it:
I lost my own cane and
started using his.

She laughs wickedly,
conspiratorially:
Everybody notices it
and gives me a seat!

— *Beverley West*

Webster Wedged it Between Serene and Serenade

The clipped clatter
of serendipity
dances a jig
on a four-leaf-clover
because
what are the chances?

Though you can't pursue it
like prospectors seek gold
it pops into view
unexpectedly
as a rainbow.

Is it coincidence
it rhymes with nobility,
when coined
from Persian tales
of three Princes from *Serendip
who discover surprising
treasures by chance?

— Nancy Taylor

**Sri Lanka, formerly known as Ceylon, formerly known as
Serendip*

Baby

A baby crawls
over the ledge
of a second-story window

I sprint across a lawn
then another
vault a laurel hedge

throw myself the last yards
land on my back
arms outstretched

my spine cracks
as I hit the brick patio
the baby slides through my arms
bounces on my chest

falls back against my knees
squeals Mama
her glass eyes
click shut.

— *Beverley West*

My First Bidet: March, 1952

Voilá—my first bidet,
aboard the *Ile de France*—
white, ceramic,
almost like an American toilet
but shallow.

Suzette explains:
"You turn the tap
and the water
swirls around.
You wash yourself every time you pee."
She reddens,
"I put on a little perfume."

"Then what?" I ask.

"My husband says,
when he throws me down on the bed
on a Saturday afternoon,

'Suzette, it's always so sweet
I could kiss it.'"

Only twenty-four
but I know
I will certainly marry a Frenchman.

—*Beverley West*

The Magic Closet

My closet is a magic act
that changes every year,
what once fit oh so perfectly
now has me in tears.

It takes my clothes and alters them,
right before my eyes;
I lift them off the hanger
then poof—a smaller size.

I talk to the magician
ask him to leave them be,
but he just keeps on his magic act
and won't tell me the key.

—Diane Moser

I LOVE the Goodwill

buy whatever I want
without looking at the price tag.

I went in for a backpack—
came out with three seaters, a velvet jacket
and a green, multi-zippered backpack.

Bob who bought a pair of cords—
not three but one—
is contemplating a backpack.

Home is the problem—
I use three-quarters of the closet space and
all the bureau drawers but one—

most of the hall closet
and shelves of the
office cubbyhole as well.

My friend Linda has
a three-story house with
a walk-in closet all her own—

there's even air space between the hangers.
Her Rule: "Buy one thing—
another goes to the Goodwill."

I try but really… we all know that
after seven years
everything comes back in style.

—*Beverley West*

Taking the Couch to the Dump

Eric—a young poet from Thursday's workshop,
hoists one end of the couch.
"It's heavy—150 pounds," he says
"would bend my hand truck.

I better call Lee
maybe he can help.
Used to be a mover."

Next day they walk in together.
I tell him I've changed my mind—
think I'll keep the couch.
"Beverley," Eric says softly
"We've already unhinged the door."

"Well OK," I say.
Lee's got rope
to tie up the couch,
slide it to the square dolly.

They roll it across the dining room floor,
juggle it onto the porch,
then to their truck.

"You're quick," I call to Eric.
"Here's extra
for the gas."

He lumbers back from the truck.
"Thanks. We'll split it 50-50."

"Oh, and Bev,
don't mention where we met.
I don't want Lee to know
I write poetry."

—*Beverley West*

Out on a Limb-erick.

Have you ever seen a Great Blue Heron
look for places to have an affair in?
With legs, neck, and wings
stretched out like strings,
he lands in an old tree that's barren.

He flies like a pterodactyl
which females find very attractyl.
He's a lean sex machine,
if you know what I mean,
with his long, sharp-pointed bill.

Watching for neighborhood dogs,
he searches for minnows and frogs.
He postures, he waits,
mainly trolling for dates
while standing stone still in the bog.

Please watch the Great Blue from a distance.
With lovers, he needs no assistance.
He'll jump on and peck 'em
and try not to wreck 'em,
yet finds not one bit of resistance.

The moral of this story I've forgotten,
my old brain resembling soft cotton.
But when wild birds in a tree
start making whoopee, just trust
that they're both besotten.

—*Adelia Ritchie*

One Hell of a Villanelle

A villanelle about writing a villanelle

The first time you write a villanelle,
you'll master the form—but not outright—
it's a poetry form that's straight out of hell.

Do it just once, and then say farewell!
Accept the challenge, get over your fright
the first time you write a villanelle.

Your rhythms are awkward, rhymes just won't gel!
You'll ponder all evening, stay up all night,
it's a poetry form that's straight out of hell.

There's no excuse if you feel unwell.
Just finish the job and you'll be alright
the first time you write a villanelle.

Your writing goes smoother with good zinfandel.
You're getting the rhymes down, keeping it tight.
It's a poetry form that's straight out of hell.

Don't give up yet! You're doing so well!
You'll use all your paper and all your graphite
the first time you write a villanelle,
this poetry form that's straight out of hell.

—*Adelia Ritchie*

GAIA

Rainfall silently
caresses the fallen leaves
winter on the way
—Diane Moser

Euterpe
Greek Muse of Lyrical Poetry

Inspire me where garter snakes hide,
cicadas click tymbals, and cedar lends scent.
Perch me where turtles
risk crossing lichen-covered logs
and ideas spring from a rabbit's hop
or the ribbit of a frog.
Where metaphor floats in the wake
of drake and mallard,
I'll ring sonnets from lady slipper tongues
and reflect rainbow from trout
to color my verse. There, as music blows
through common reed, I'll mark tempo
with a cattail wand. When thought
doesn't stream like a minnow school,
I'll find patience in a heron's pose.

—*Nancy Taylor*

Perspective

When the Harvest Moon nods
to winter, spider webs
hold my house hostage.
Aspen trees glitter in gold
until leaves and temperatures
drop. While embracing autumn,

I dread winter when incessant
rain prompts me to consider
Prozac. My neighbor stops
delivering fresh eggs. His chickens
don't like this latitude at year's end either.

Since winter has not besieged us yet,
I toss faded flowers into compost,
ready bird feeders, and cut a handful
of dahlias. The squirrels scurry
their treasure over the fence
and give me perspective.

—Nancy Taylor

An Apology to the Bee

In my previous ode
I lambasted you—
for good cause.
There, I detailed
dates and locations
you and your ilk attacked me—
an innocent bystander,
car rider, picnicker,
tent putter-upper.
You even stung my dog!

But I want you in my garden
where you can waggle dance
with hive mates
and double my crop.
To prove no grudges,
I'll plant flowers for me
and my bees.

— *Nancy Taylor*

Earth is my Element

While I balance happy
        in yin
with worry
        in yang,
it's challenging
to worry happily.

However, my nature
        is to nurture—
babysitting in my teens,
30-year nursing career

and now I cheer seeds
into vegetables.

Sadly, this summer,
        my leaves mimic
Swiss cheese,
while beans
        and carrot tops vanish.

I watch two mice
export strawberries
        from my netted bed.

When Sluggo loses war
        with slugs,
I try beer—for the slugs.

While often critters eat
        more than I,
I persist in planting

because fresh earth
        is my incense,
because I dig
        watching tiny seeds
sprout into big leafy plants,

because it helps me stay
        balanced.

—Nancy Taylor

Manitou Bay Wonderland

Diamonds dance
on the salty water
dressing white Seagulls in jewels.

They respond with
a thank you
for making them queen.

Dipping and diving
in royal formation
a perfect blend

of courtly maneuvers
calling out to the salmon
"off with your heads."

—*Diane Moser*

Rapture

The clear, cool
flow of water
carries me downstream.
Cedar trees along the bank
look down in envy.

Clouds smile a wish
to join my journey.
Shiny river stones
gently kissed by current
watch me pass.

A boulder, century-smooth
gently brushes my body.
I pass deep pools
where forest critters
come to drink.

Sounds blend into river
and wind tiptoes
through the forest.
Rhythm sings a tune
of tomorrow

and tomorrow.

— *Diane Moser*

Along Rich Passage

cormorants
guard
pier pilings

sea lions
honking
their
songs

seven geese
soar
high
above

through
silver
gray
swirling
skies

—*Sue Hylen*

early morning rains

spit
splattering
melodies

through
dry grasses
&
dead leaves

birthing
acorns
into
trees

—*Sue Hylen*

Fort Ward Trail

Broad leaf maples
cedar
fir
stretch
up
through
afternoon
shadows
along
this
emerald
bronze
forest
trail

sanctifying
dying
light

—*Sue Hylen*

Six Ravens

soar
over
West Port Madison
shores

dance
dive
through
thunderhead
clouds

ebony
wings
glisten

through
swirling
stormy
skies

—Sue Hylen

The Grand Forest

Cedar
trunks
curl & stretch
tall
with
tips
of
hemlock and fir.

Alder leaves
glisten
green
above
sword ferns
dancing
with
unexpected breezes.

Stumps
and
burls
smile
back at me
as
I walk over
twigs & stones

dirt
dry as dust
above a river
of
roots
through
this
Forest to Sky
Trail.

—*Sue Hylen*

Through My Spyglass

Last chick to leave,
wings flapping for weeks now,
he peers over the edge of
his enormous nest of sticks—
sticks that seem to have been thrown in air
yet somehow fallen into the elbow of this cedar
in a hectic manner and yet an appropriate shape.

Looks as if he is saying, *no way,*
then with one hop back to center nest
preening his feathers, flapping
and flapping
and flapping his wings—
just one more time.

Soon Eagle Mother will toss
from the nest those shells, those bone toys
she brought to fill his chick time.
Now it's time for that next step—
into midair.

      —Dawn Henthorn

Little Stream

Your quiet trickle moves
over soft ground from
a still-water puddle of a pool.

Gravity pulls you forward, down,
over shale rock steps,
tumbling onward,
passing through dark
Sitka spruce woods
dressed in thick, downy moss
out into grey skies, mist—
then sunshine.

Onward down the hillside
sharing this stream with
living creatures—
plain sticklebacks,
dazzling blue dragonflies,
long-legged water skippers—
until this little stream,
protected and safe in its edges,
dumps out into
dark waters of the lake—
unique no more,
melded with the whole.

—*Dawn Henthorn*

A Pregnant Spring

Butterflies, honey bees, bumble bees
will be here soon—

feverfew, borage, zinnias poking through,
I'm bent digging weeds from dark warm earth,
sun soaks its way into my back.

Unseen birds twitter in the trees
having found a mate urgently they build their nests—
back and forth, back and forth.

Soft coos of neighbor chickens
scratch earth finding
seeds, worms, bugs.

A lovely respite of a day
as I stretch out in the smell
of green, of grass, of earth—

maybe I'll go in after this lazy cloud
makes it over those mountains.

—Dawn Jarvela Henthorn

COMPANIONS

Children run at play
fall into golden leaves
dog loves the action.
—Diane Moser

One Must Have a Mind of Dogs

to understand how they live
in the moment
like Buddhist monks,

to understand their quality of life
is heightened by their senses—
sniffing wet spots,
tasting bone marrow,
relishing tummy rubs.

While tails wag
to convey their moods,
don't expect to hide yours—

they get you.

        —Nancy Taylor

Bait

The barred owl hoots, *who cooks for you,*
from the neighboring forest.
I scurry my toy dogs out of its view.

Next, the owl hoots the monkey tune
I heard while serving Bolivia's poorest.
The barred owl hoots, *who cooks for you,*

with the bluesy voice of Madeline Peyroux
serenades without a chorus.
I scurry my toy dogs out of its view.

It perches on our fence beside a Yew
gawking like a tourist.
The barred owl hoots, *who cooks for you.*

It must be starving, the sky is blue.
What havoc have humans bore us
I scurry my toy dogs out of its view.

Two owls fly past our house to pursue
a rabbit beneath their orbit.
The barred owl hoots, *who cooks for you.*
I scurry my toy dogs out of its view.

—*Nancy Taylor*

104

It's Not About Pluto

When I tell Justin I love him past Pluto
he tilts his head, his lexicon supplies
only treats and names or places, and so
I say Pluto lies farther than a ball can fly.
Then add, Pluto shares world sovereignty
with brothers Zeus, who reigns over the sky,
and Poseidon, who rules over the sea,
but neither does a planet signify.
While Pluto, god of the underworld, presides
not only over afterlife, but future times,
underground, where minerals hide
and seeds are stored in bountiful mines.
When I consider Pluto the cartoon,
my Justin no longer looks attuned.

—*Nancy Taylor*

Rejoicing in Justin

Inspired by Christopher Smart, "Jubilate Agno"

For I will consider my dog Justin, whose fur, unrivaled in softness,
floats as manna from heaven.

For unlike Lot's wife, he doesn't look back;
he knows the wonders of his world lie ahead.

For he is an extrovert, wriggling his tail and barking
if needed until greeted.

For his nature is forgiving; he licks me when
I step on him.

For he is patient, spurning hunger and thirst,
he window-waits for my return.

For he is a gentleman dog, allowing his sister
first dibs at the kibble bowl.

For he honors ancestors by howling moonward
when playing with cousin Inky.

For cleanliness meets holiness as he
licks paws after a walk.

For his dark black-lined eyes, study me
from sofa armrest where he props his chin.

For attentive listening grows his vocabulary:
brush teeth, park, let's go excite him.

For he is always reverent, bowing to opponents before
pouncing in play.

For our daily walks turn serene, sniffing scent

106

from each sprig of heath.

For he moves like a sannyasin, stretching each vertebra
in turn upon rising.

For routines suit him, when my electric toothbrush buzzes
he trots to the bathroom to await his turn.

For he obeys mundane commands: sit, shake, stay, unless
a deer catches his eye.

For his petting quota swelled after telling him
he's my true love.

—*By Nancy Taylor*

Apology to My Pet Sitter

Inspired by Rebecca Foust, "Apology to my OB/Gyn"

Sorry Koukla wouldn't eat
while I was away. I showed you
how to feed her. She takes time,
I said—but you were too impatient.

Sorry she peed on the carpet
when you wouldn't let her out.
She's old and cannot see and
didn't know how to tell you.

Sorry you wouldn't let me
take her to her litter-mate's house.
They love her there and understand.
Sorry I had to leave her with you

but you insisted. She'll be fine now,
she's gaining weight, letting me
brush her mats out when you wouldn't.
She licked my nose to say she's sorry too.

—*Adelia Ritchie*

108

Uncle Earl's Menagerie

"Come see the dancing mice," he said,
as they lined up on cue—
thoughts of cheese reward
dancing in their heads.

A tightrope hung between two chairs,
anticipation in the air.
The rodents with tiny feet,
tails like lamp cords—
stepped out
and balanced in line, across possibilities.

I held my breath.
The thrill of discovery
in my child heart.

—Diane Moser

Gus and Me

I watch him sit,
commanding identity,
his rounded mass
of fur and pride
though wanting love
does turn away
to lick, to preen,
to gather balance,
to wait.

I watch him sleep
stretched soft
that fluid mass of vulnerability;
yet do I see uneasy dreams
that twitch and curl
the whiskered mouth,
that cast a shadow
on primitive pleasure?

I watch him play,
quick darts of energy
released to unseen calls;
soft batting pads
in imitative combat,
arched back against invisible foe.

I watch him age,
the white ear tufts,
a cautious stretch
slowed down in weary bones,
asking no new consideration
finds survival in detachment.

—Diane Moser

I knew

when very young
I had a soft, mushy heart
for the underdog—
the kitten missing an eye,
the runt of the litter,
the broken-winged,
the less perfect.

Perfect seems to go
against nature.

Perfect seems
overrated.

—Dawn Henthorn

Rrrrromance

She could tell by his random stacking
of sticks and uncut rounds
he knew little about building a wood fire.
Raised in the country
alongside an intelligent pig,
she wondered if his city ways
would divide them.

Her eyes, large and brown, her hair long and fluffy—
his, shaggy, whitish, shedding
on the navy blue chair
next to the fireplace.
She approached on all fours,
submissive, murmuring softly.
"Rrrrrrr…," he growled, invitingly.

—Adelia Ritchie

BACKROOM

The hills are on fire
embers shoot into the air
politicians stall
—Diane Moser

When the News Steals Joy

I draw my dreams
      with magic markers
            on our TV screen.

When the news steals joy
      I roll out my yoga mat
            through morning clouds of doubt.

When the news steals joy
      I pedal my bicycle
            passing cars stuck in traffic

turn right along Manitou Beach Drive
      where cormorants perch
            on tall pier pilings

where sunlight glistens
      beyond Puget Sound
            through Glacier Peak Wilderness skies.

      —Sue Hylen

First They'll Come for the Journalists

First, they'll come for the journalists.
They'll toss them in jail like murder suspects,
but those lying meddlers won't be missed.

Writers, reporters, and cartoonists—
then atheists, leftists, and network execs—
but first they'll come for the journalists.

Science and data, officials insist,
have no bearing on climate effects.
Those lying reporters won't be missed.

Physicians, teachers, and scientists,
their threat to this government is more complex,
but first, they'll come for the journalists.

If the media is lying, does truth exist?
They'll get 'em for treason or other pretext.
Those fact-checking meddlers won't be missed.

Now handcuffed and gagged, they no longer resist
And we don't know what happened next.
First, they came for the journalists
Those lying meddlers won't be missed.

—*Adelia Ritchie*

The Battle Hymn

Attacked globally by unseen
invaders we fight an enemy
invisible as birdsong,
omnipresent as sound,
mute as a *tacet*.

This new foe whispers
pianissimo in some people,
blares *forte* in others.

Our nation needs a conductor
to orchestrate fifty states
to play to the same beat,
with rhapsody—notes rising
till there are no further cries
for testing supplies or PPE.

Then we'll synchronize
beyond the crest
when the world is less
careening and we all share
a vaccine.

—*Nancy Taylor*

American Treaties

The sun lays hot and endless
over the dusty desert reservation.
A sad, scruffy dog
struggles to find shade.

Outside the weather-worn hogan
bleached grey by years of dry heat,
a little girl sits
struggles to pedal her toddler trike,
despite a broken spoke,
bent axle and flat tire.

She rocks back and forth
back and forth
over and over,
gets off and tries to push it
over the dust-layered ground.

No whining, no complaint
she knows already
her small voice
will not be heard.

—*Diane Moser*

Customs Confiscates Rosaries

Two young Guatemalan women quietly ask for rosaries
placed on a give-away table
with toiletries, barrettes, and hair bands.

One caresses the gift in her palm,
the other clenches the delicate chain
joining cross with beads,

replacing the talismans they used
to seek guidance from above
while GPS guided their smuggler's path.

　　　—Nancy Taylor

CLIMATE

jungle denizens
petri dish for pathogens
it's so warm today
—Adelia Ritchie

Through the Rippled Glass

of civilization
I see the land.
It floats above, below, around
telling stories
we do not hear.

The beached whale, eyes
rolled back forever knows.
The queen bee surrounded by
her dead workers knows.
A million jellyfish drying
in porous sand all know.

We in our arrogance
our dominion over all,
ignore what is right before us
too self-involved
to see the signs.

—Diane Moser

The Amazon Burns

The Amazon burns—it's not in our news
though ten million species call it home.
What about the Howler monkeys' views?

This canopied lung our planet will lose
when we destroy rainforest's biome.
The Amazon burns—it's not in our news.

Impunity sparks land grabber abuse,
who deforest then burn logs for ashen loam.
What about jaguars' and pumas' views?

Jungles are converted into grassland hues,
logging and mining tear plant rhizomes.
The Amazon burns—it's not in our news.

Pleas for beef and leather light this fuse,
farmers profit more where cattle roam.
What about the Yanomami's views?

Demise of carbon-sinking trees incurs dues
returns it back to gas, depletes ozone.
The Amazon burns—it's not in our news.
What about the next generation's views?

—Nancy Taylor

Once

I remember fishing
in a 40-foot-deep lake so clear

I thought I could touch pebbles
lining the bottom.

Then a child could eat
walleye, perch and bass daily.

Today, northern Minnesota lakes
harbor mercury, dioxin, other toxins.

A child may eat one
fish serving per month.

And the pebbles hide.

—Nancy Taylor

Water
what the next wars will be about

damp moist dewy wet
humid steaming sticky sweat
rain hail sleet snow
fog mist cloud rainbow

brook river creek stream
pond lake ocean sea
raft boat surfboard ski
thunderstorm waterspout tsunami

cyclone typhoon hurricane
wild northeaster wind-wave train
ice liquid vapor slush
flow drip burble gush

torrent rapids waterfall
glacier iceberg plump snowball
drink bathe swim splash shower
sprinkle it on a bright red flower.

—Adelia Ritchie

Editor's note: Adelia and Dawn were driving home from Poetry Workshop one afternoon when they noticed a new clearcut alongside the road. They challenged each other to write a poem with the identical title, "Where the Woods Were," and these are the results!

Where the Woods Were

ferns
mushrooms
spruce-needle carpet
stickleback stream
hillside backyard
treehouse dreams
memories under paved roads
cement house footings
fences
gates

moss-covered lean-tos
made of fallen branches
hiding dozens
of white surveyor's stakes
deep in the woods

now a childhood memory—
two shy, sweet,
no-trouble-at-all little girls
now two grown guilty women and—
a crime never solved

—Dawn Henthorn

Where the Woods Were

An ode to a lost forest

Where the woods were
a trillium bloomed
in the shade
of an ancient
cedar tree

snowberries peeked
through branches
stealing sunlight
from mosses

sword ferns unfurled
green wings
fanned out
from hairy backbones

tiny shrew families
dug earthworms
woodpeckers
and wood ducks
made nests
in knotholes

salamanders slithered
where deer hooves trod
raccoons played
and cougars roared

where the woods were.

—*Adelia Ritchie*

Survival

Lost on a beach in the Aleutians
you can catch a seagull
with a safety pin and a line.
Pack with mud and seaweed
roast in a bed of hot rocks.
Feathers come off with the mud.

Lost in the frozen north
melt snow
drink tree bark tea
lay branches on snow
in an SOS.

How does one get rescued from fear?
Where are the bark, the line, the branches?

—*Dawn Henthorn*

PALETTE

when tulips erupt
springtime pronounces pretty
my heart sings happy
—Nancy Taylor

Ode to Red

don't doubt your status—
        you color Oscar's carpet
you glisten in garnets and rubies
        you title a sea that parted

while Santa chose you for his favorite color,
nature chooses you—
        to feather cardinals and woodpecker heads
        to reveal when a pepper's most sweet
        to tint Lincoln roses

in summer you smell like ripe strawberries
and at the movie counter, Red Hots

in fall you flame Burning Bushes
then cherry-nosed children who squeal
in the snow

though you're anything but gentle,
known for a temper,
consider your connotation for life:
        blood circulates to oxygenate our bodies
        corner signs, Stop!
        fire engines carry heroes
            who brave hotter and hotter flames

women over fifty wear scarlet hats with pride,
if you asked one to dance, you'd tango, pivoting
and dipping, long-stemmed red rose in mouth

    —Nancy Taylor

Ode to Yellow

Though Donovan bound you to mellow
for the rhyme—*they call me mellow yellow…*

to many you imply a start—
sunrise, pollen, dandelion—first flower for bees.

You ruffle daffodils in parades
and preschoolers focus when

neon Big Bird teaches lessons on kindness.
Lest you get cocky, you signal deceit

in some journalism. However, on No. 2 pencils
you aim to mark Scantrons correctly.

When you caution at stop lights,
drivers try to abide.

The Beatles' "Yellow Submarine" curses
an earworm—*we all live in a yellow submarine…*

You, and Aphrodite signified
love in Ancient Greece.

As a firefly and sometimes a comet,
you flaunt your superpower.

You highlight when bananas ripen
and stink up rotten eggs.

Speaking of eggs, you connote
chicken, as in yellow-bellied coward.

—Nancy Taylor

Ode to Green

Don't worry about your association
with envy. You should know
everyone wants—
> you in their wallets,
> you at the stoplight,
> you on their lawns.

Nature chooses you a favorite color—
> to pigment chlorophyll,
> paint the forest canopy,
> color quetzals neon green

Though you dominate in foliage,
in flower beds you hold back,
allow roses their show.
You susurrate when wind
whooshes grass and leaves.

In green tea, we taste your essence
and inhale your punch with vetiver,
mint, and thyme.

Your shades display worldwide—
> Korean celadon vases,
> Columbian emeralds,
> deep green Canadian conifers.

Hawaiian Islands wear your color.
There, you dance the hula, shaking
a grass skirt like a dog leaving a lake.

—*Nancy Taylor*

Orange Epiphany

No one writes a poem
about the color orange.
Or the fruit orange.
Or the aging hooker, having seen
the inside of too many smoky bars, who asks,
"Orange you going to come see me sometime?"

Orange is a lively, warm, attractive color—
attention-getting, friendly. Also a warning—
don't come any closer!
Like a flame—beckoning, compelling,
but safe only at a distance.

To Isaac Newton—a synesthetic—
orange was the color of the key of D.
A beam of light passing through his prism
must have looked to him like a concert
at the Royal Albert Hall.

Orange once was the color of sunrise,
a robin's breast, a field of ripe pumpkins,
the Lamborghini of my wet dreams.
These days I see orange as the color
of Satan's testicles roasting over the fires of hell.

And now I know that orange is dishonest.
It's not even its own color at all,
but rather the blending of red and yellow,

primary colors that married,
gave birth to orange,
and haven't spoken since.

Orange is an angry lava flow,
an old-growth forest incinerating itself,

the glowing eyes of a stalking demon at midnight.

Orange is everywhere, a terrifying tsunami
of hatred and destruction.

This is why I'm so blue.

    —Adelia Ritchie

Rethinking Pink

Pink bedroom for baby girl
can change the way she thinks—
pretty in pink
lipstick and tutus
titty pink—
it's all pink inside

Pink paints one naïve,
inexperienced, youthful—
cotton candy,
bubble gum,
strawberry milkshakes

We like pink animals—
flamingos,
piglets,
coral

and pink flowers—
pinks,
roses,
camellias

and things to eat
with our pink tongues—
watermelon,
ham,
salmon

Pepto-Bismol keeps us
in the pink
as we wield pinking shears
to make a sawtooth edge
on baby pink fabrics

Pink can calm
but not for long,
can enrage prisoners
kept in pink rooms—

enrages *me* to recall
my childhood bedroom—
pink roses on green wallpaper
and pink chenille bedspread

Yet that pink commode
and vanity sink
in Nancy Rekow's house
on Tuesday afternoons—

I must rethink
how much I hate
the color pink.

—Adelia Ritchie

Accidental Masterpiece

Green arm
with red fingers
swims sideways
through crazy-quilt flotsam—
bright swishes of blue
yellow, turquoise, pink

blue fish glide
through pink yellow
blue seaweed
in crowded tide pools

swoops, drips, stabs
stripes, dots. strokes—
a cacophony of colors
accidental

my watercolor
pigment test strip
a masterpiece
of abstraction

—*Adelia Ritchie*

Acknowledgements

"Anna," by Diane Moser, winner of Matter Oprelle Publications poetry contest, 2024.

"Hard to Lee!" by Sue Hylen, originally published in *Spindrift Art & Literary Journal*, 2019, and *Lines from My Notebooks,* self-published in 2020.

"While Knitting a Cable Knit Sweater," by Sue Hylen, originally published in *"Spindrift Art & Literary Journal,"* 2019, and *"Lines from My Notebooks,"* self-published in 2020.

"What's in a Name," by Nancy Taylor, originally published in *"Last Stanza Journal,"* issue:10, 2022.

"September 28, 1991," by Sue Hylen, originally published in *Spillway,* 1994, and in *"Double Exposure,"* self-published in 2001.

"My Muse," by Sue Hylen, originally published in *"Spindrift Art & Literary Journal,"* 2019.

"*While waiting to read my Seattle Metro Bus Poems at the Elliott Bay Book Store,"* by Sue Hylen, originally published in *"Seattle Metro Bus Poetry Competition."*

"Double Exposure," by Sue Hylen, originally published in *"Double Exposure,"* self-published in 2001.

"Midwinter, New Hampshire, 1967," by Sue Hylen, originally published in *"Double Exposure,"* self-published in 2001, first appeared in *"Stone Country Spring/Summer Poetry Journal,"* 1989.

"She Wasn't Young," by Adelia Ritchie, first appeared in *"Poetry Corners 2022,"* a publication of Poetry Corners.

"Older Lovers," by Beverley West, published in *"Let's Always Miss Our Flight,"* self-published, 2019.

"A Late Romance," by Beverley West, published in *"Let's Always Miss Our Flight,"* self-published, 2019.

"Sometimes I Wonder," by Adelia Ritchie, first appeared in *"MATTER, Award-winning Poetry,"* published by Oprelle Publications LLC, 2020.

"On the Bus Seattle, 1990," by Beverley West, published in *"Let's Always Miss Our Flight,"* self-published, 2019.

"My First Bidet: March, 1952," by Beverley West, published in *"Let's Always Miss Our Flight,"* self-published, 2019.

"I LOVE the Goodwill," by Beverley West, published in *"Let's Always Miss Our Flight,"* self-published, 2019.

"Taking the Couch to the Dump," by Beverley West, published in *"Let's Always Miss Our Flight,"* self-published, 2019.

"Euterpe," by Nancy Taylor, originally published in *"Minnow Literary Journal,"* Winter 21/22.

"Perspective," by Nancy Taylor, first appeared in *"Women Writing: On the Edge of Dark and Light,"* published by Pilgrim Spirit Communications, 2015.

"Earth is my Element," by Nancy Taylor, first appeared in *"Wingless Dreamer-Anthology: A Garden of Poets,"* 2022.

"Manitou Bay Wonderland," by Diane Moser, first appeared in Ars Poetica 2001.

"Fort Ward Trail," by Sue Hylen, originally published in *"Poetry Corners 2022,"* Bainbridge Island Arts & Humanities Council.

"One must have a mind of dogs," by Nancy Taylor, originally published in *"Can We Keep Him?"* self-published, 2018.

"Rejoicing in Justin," by Nancy Taylor, originally published in *"Last Stanza Journal,"* issue #15, 2023.

"First They'll Come for the Journalists," by Adelia Ritchie, first appeared in *"Poetry Corners 2022,"* a publication of Poetry Corners.

"The Battle Hymn," by Nancy Taylor, originally published in *"The Literary Nest,"* vol.6, issue 2.

"American Treaties," by Diane Moser, short-listed for the 2024 poetry contest, Matter Oprelle Publications, 2024.

"Through the Rippled Glass," by Diane Moser, originally published in *"Civilization in Crisis,"* published by Foothills Publishing, 2021.

"The Amazon Burns," by Nancy Taylor, originally published in *"The Literary Nest Journal,"* vol. #6, issue 3, 2020.

"Once," by Nancy Taylor, first appeared in *"Civilization in Crisis: An Anthology of Poetic Response,"* by FootHills Publishing, 2021.

"Water," by Adelia Ritchie, first appeared in *"Ars Poetica,"* 2019.

"Where the Woods Were," by Adelia Ritchie, originally published in *"Salish Magazine,"*
Winter 2023.

MEET THE AUTHORS

Pens dance on pages
voices woven through the years
hearts in quiet bloom
—Adelia Ritchie

Dawn Jarvela Henthorn

Dawn Henthorn grew up in Kodiak, Alaska, during the impressionable ages of 3-20. The smells, sights, and nature of the island, along with the sturdy, gentle, generous, gregarious nature of its people, indelibly influenced her art, writing, and personality. Dawn sculpts in clay and soapstone and is currently working on her memoir about growing up on Kodiak.

Dawn's career as a writer includes two rejections and three "exposures." Her poem *Stranded* was exhibited in Poetry Corners 2006, sponsored by BIAHC. For years, Dawn regularly participated in Nancy Rekow's writing group, *"learning to be brave as I learn to write."* She has read for Poetry Corners from 2014-2018 and contributed to the chapbook anthology, *Ode to Nancy Rekow,* assembled by her former students.

Since leaving Kodiak Island in the mid-60s, the Pacific Northwest has been her home. Dawn has lived in Kingston for the past 35 years with one old dog and husband, John.

Sue Hylen

Sue Hylen, a poet and photographer, finds images with her pen and lens in those unexpected juxtaposed moments while walking a forest trail or playing with her 6 grandchildren. In 1987 Sue met Nancy Rekow who invited her to attend the Thursday evening Bainbridge Island Writers workshop where she began to find her muse. In 2001, Sue published her first chapbook, *Double Exposure*. Upon her retirement in 2017 from the Bainbridge Island Metro Park District after 30 years as the Cultural Arts Manager, Sue published her second chapbook, *Lines from My Notebooks*. In 2022, Sue published *Unravelling My Life Lines*, her first full length book of poems, dedicated to Nancy Rekow.

Diane Moser

Diane lives on the Kitsap Peninsula overlooking the beautiful Olympic Mountains, where a lifetime of observation is reflected in her poetry.

She feels words can connect in a time when we need to hear and understand each other. Diane is grateful for this unexpected gift of words that have helped her navigate the last chapter of life. She hopes you find a sense of connection and shared experience in her poetry.

Adelia Ritchie, PhD

Adelia Ritchie is a scientist, artist, and recovering technical writer. A long-time resident of the Pacific Northwest, her writings are inspired by her travels, her paintings, and her love for the interesting and unusual. Her poems and nature articles have been published in *Salish Magazine,* where she was a contributing editor.

Her recent book, *The Accidental Expat: A Costa Rican Adventure,* was inspired by her adventures in setting up a household in Costa Rica, where she currently resides. Her newest book of poems, *An Accidental Masterpiece,* is in press and will be available in the Fall of 2024.

Nancy Taylor

Nancy Taylor has been "arranging words" since she retired from a long nursing career. Occasionally her words come out poetic, other times they cue up in crosswords. She enjoys the way poetry forces her to examine things carefully, focus on imagery, and explain with clarity.

Her poetry book, *Can We Keep Him*, was written to benefit Kitsap Animal Rescue & Education (K.A.R.E.), a local animal rescue organization. She enjoys traveling, gardening, playing with Benji, her fluffy black Havipoo, and walking among cedars in the Pacific Northwest where she lives on an island with her husband.

Beverley Lehman West

Beverley West is a transplanted San Franciscan. She lived in Paris and New York before settling on Bainbridge Island in 1977. She has worked as a reporter for the San Francisco Chronicle and as an ESL instructor at Seattle Central College. Her poems and stories have appeared in regional journals as well as in an early chapbook, *For All the Wrong Reasons*. Beverley's recent memoir, *Finding My Way Back to 1950s Paris*, is about a young San Franciscan going to Paris in the 50s, living in a garret, studying French, writing in cafes on the Left Bank, listening to jazz in dank caves, and of course, falling in love a few times. The memoir was a finalist for the 2015 Nancy Pearl Book Award of the Pacific Northwest Writers Association.

Bev's most recent book, *"Let's Always Miss Our Flight,"* published in 2019, is her contagious and inspiring memoir in poetry, full of humor and heartbreak. In 69 prose poems, West time-travels through her youth, treating the reader to some of her most popular and risqué poems, set in San Francisco, Paris and New York.

She has two sons, raised in San Francisco and on Bainbridge, and four grandchildren.

www.ingramcontent.com/pod-product-compliance
Lightning Source LLC
Chambersburg PA
CBHW051524120626
46551CB00012B/1063